MAKING SCIENCE WORK

Floating
and
Sailing

TERRY JENNINGS

Illustrations by
Peter Smith and
Catherine Ward

RSVP

**RAINTREE
STECK-VAUGHN**
P U B L I S H E R S
The Steck-Vaughn Company

Austin, Texas

Published by Raintree Steck-Vaughn Publishers, an imprint of Steck-Vaughn Company

A Mirabel Book

Produced by Cynthia Parzych Publishing, Inc.
648 Broadway, New York, NY 10012

Designed by Arcadia Consultants

Printed and bound in Spain by International Graphic Service

1 2 3 4 5 6 7 8 9 0 pl 99 98 97 96 95

Library of Congress Cataloging-in-Publication Data
Jennings, Terry J.
    Floating and sailing / Terry Jennings ; illustrations by Peter Smith and Catherine Ward.
        p.   cm. — (Making science work)
    "A Mirabel book."
    Includes index
    ISBN 0–8172–3958–8
    ISBN 0–8172–4251–1 (softcover)
    1. Displacement (Ships)—Juvenile literature.   2. Sailing—Juvenile literature.
3. Floating bodies—Juvenile literature.   [1. Displacement (Ships)   2. Sailing.   3. Floating bodies.
4. Water—Experiments.   5. Experiments.]   I. Smith, Peter, 1948– ill.   II. Ward, Catherine, ill.
III. Title. IV. Series: Jennings, Terry J.   Making science work
    VM157.J46   1996
    532'.2—dc20   95–6000
                                                                                      CIP
                                                                                       AC

Key to Symbols

"See for Yourself" element

Demonstrates the principles of the subject

Warning! Adult help is required

Activity for the child to try

Contents

Boats and Ships 4

Early Boats 6

Rafts 8

Sail Power – See for Yourself 10

Build a Catamaran – See for Yourself 12

Floating and Sinking – See for Yourself 14

Why Do Big Things Float? – See for Yourself ... 16

Why Do Steel Ships Float? – See for Yourself 18

Inside a Large Ship 20

Ships and Cargo – See for Yourself 22

Hovercraft 24

Build a Model Hovercraft – See for Yourself 26

Submarines 28

Make a Submarine – See for Yourself 30

Glossary 31

Index 32

Boats and Ships

Boats and ships float on water. They come in all shapes and sizes. Very large ships can carry lots of people or things. Large ships have powerful engines to push them along. Some small boats carry only one person. They may be blown along by the wind. They may be rowed along with oars or paddles. Or they may have small engines to push them along.

Racing yacht

Cruise liner

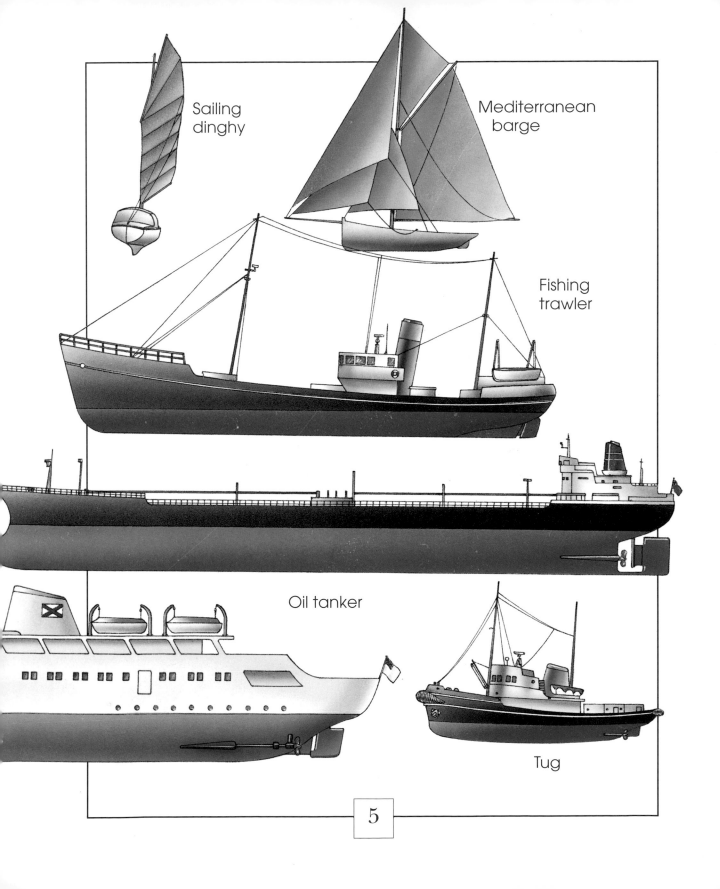

Sailing dinghy

Mediterranean barge

Fishing trawler

Oil tanker

Tug

5

Early Boats

The first boats were made from logs. A person sat on the log. He used a stick to push himself along. Then rafts were made by tying logs together. They could carry several people. Later, people hollowed out logs to make canoes.

Some people made boats from bundles of reeds. Others used sticks and animal skins. These early boats were moved by people's muscles, using paddles or oars. The first ships also had sails that were used to catch the wind. The wind blew the sails and pushed the ship along.

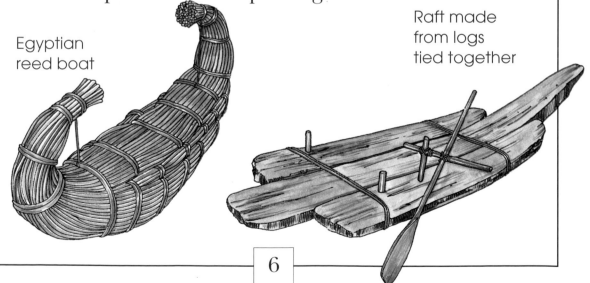

Egyptian
reed boat

Raft made
from logs
tied together

Dugout made by hollowing out a tree with an ax and fire

Coracle

7

Rafts

Rafts are still used today, but these rafts are usually made of rubber. Special life rafts are carried on ships and aircraft. They are used if there is an accident. If an airplane crashes in the sea, the rafts can be used by the people on board to escape from it. Ships carry rafts folded up in large drums. When the drum is thrown in the water, the raft fills with gas and floats. Some people use large rubber rafts for fun. They float along fast-flowing rivers in them.

An inflatable rubber raft

In 1947 a Norwegian called Thor Heyerdahl made a large raft from balsa logs. It was a model of a very old raft. The raft was called the *Kon Tiki*. Heyerdahl was able to sail more than 4,300 miles (6,923 km) across the Pacific Ocean in his raft. He sailed from Peru to the Polynesian Islands.

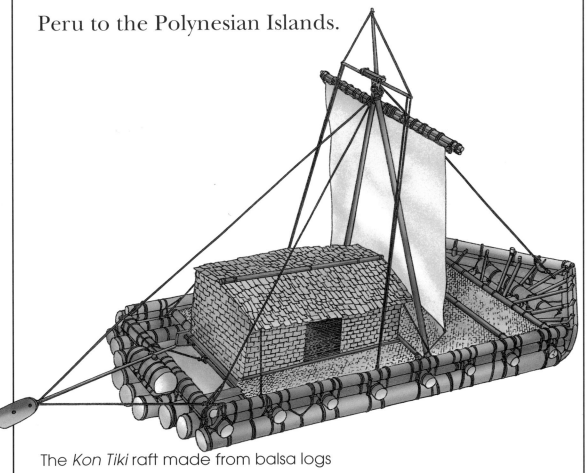

The *Kon Tiki* raft made from balsa logs

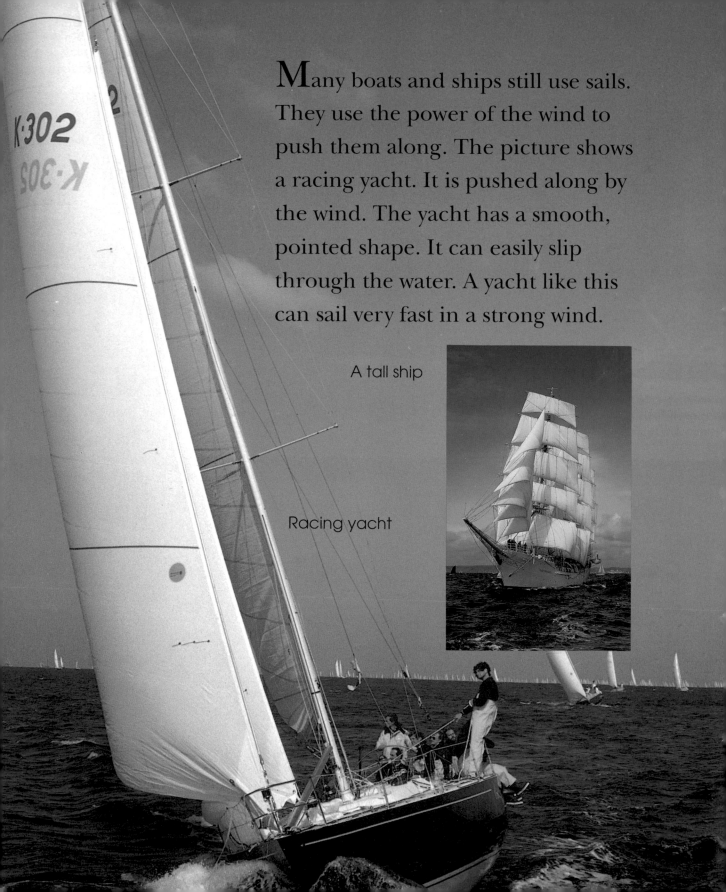

Many boats and ships still use sails. They use the power of the wind to push them along. The picture shows a racing yacht. It is pushed along by the wind. The yacht has a smooth, pointed shape. It can easily slip through the water. A yacht like this can sail very fast in a strong wind.

A tall ship

Racing yacht

Make a sailboat of your own. Cut the top off a milk carton. Press a lump of clay in the bottom. Push the paper sail onto a drinking straw. Stick the straw into the clay. Put your boat on the water. Blow into the middle of the sail. How does the boat move? Try sails of different shapes and sizes. Which works best?

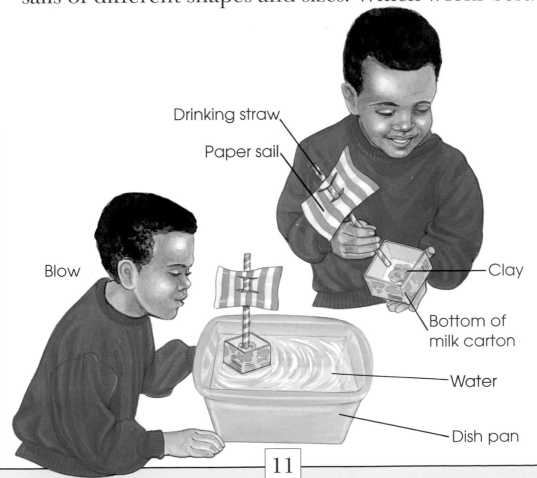

Drinking straw

Paper sail

Blow

Clay

Bottom of milk carton

Water

Dish pan

11

Build a Catamaran – See for Yourself

The part of the boat in which you sit is called the hull. Most boats and ships have only one hull. But a catamaran has two hulls.

A catamaran has two hulls.

1 Cut a plastic bottle in half.

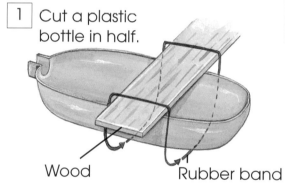

Wood

Rubber band

2 Join the halves like this.

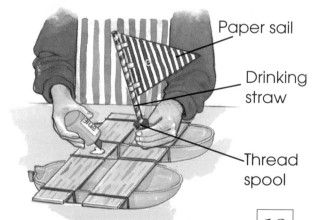

Paper sail

Drinking straw

Thread spool

Make a model catamaran. Ask an adult to help you to cut a plastic bottle down the center. Join the two halves with two small pieces of wood. Use rubber bands to hold the pieces together.

3 Test your catamaran.

Glue a thread spool to one of the pieces of wood. Attach a mast and sail to this. Test your catamaran. Which do you think would turn over most easily — a boat with one hull or a boat with two hulls?

13

Floating and Sinking
See for Yourself

Some things float on water while others sink. Collect some small objects. Can you guess which ones will float? Now test them.

Dish pan of cold water

14

Make a chart to show your results. Look at the things that float. Are they light or heavy? Are they big or small? What shapes are they? Do they all float in the same way? What will happen if you attach a thing that floats to one that sinks? Try it and see.

Why Do Big Things Float?
See for Yourself

Big ships are made of steel. Although they are very heavy, these ships float; and yet a steel washer sinks. You can see why a ship floats if you get some modeling clay. Roll the clay into a ball. Put it into a dish pan of water. See how the ball sinks. Dry the clay and make it into a boat shape. Put it in the water. It will float now.

1 Roll the modeling clay.

2 Make a boat shape.

3 Put it in cold water.

Water always seems to push upward. Put a tennis ball in a dish pan of water. Try pushing the ball under the water. What do you feel?

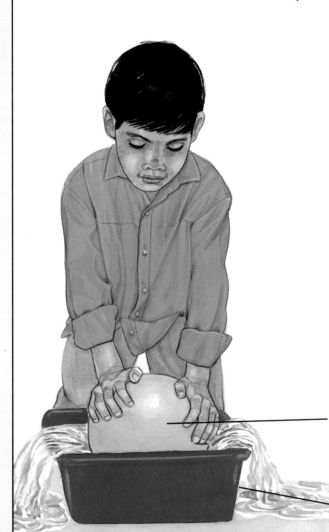

Now do this with a large rubber ball. The water seems to push back much harder. The more you push the ball down, the more the water rises up the dish pan. The ball pushes the water out of the way.

Large rubber ball

Tennis ball

Dish pan of cold water

17

Big ships are very heavy. Their steel hulls are shaped so that they push away a lot of water. The water pushes back hard against the large hull. It keeps the ship afloat.

A container ship is very heavy. It carries cargo in large boxes called containers. These are packed before being taken to the port.

A ship also floats because it is filled with air. If a lot of water gets into the ship, it will become heavier. Then it will sink. Soft drink cans are made of thin metal. Find two empty soft drink cans. Fill one can with water. Put the two cans in a dish pan of water.

Soft drink can

Dish pan of cold water

The can filled with water will sink, but the other one will float because it is lighter. Push this can underwater. Will it float or sink?

19

Large passenger ships are called ocean liners. They are built for vacation cruises. They are like floating hotels. The world's largest and longest cruise ship is the *Norway*. It was built in 1961 and is 1,035 feet (316 m) long.

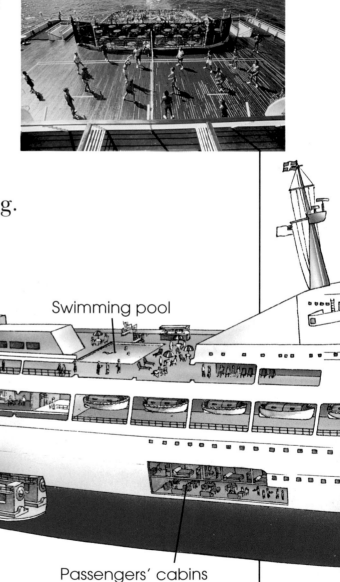

Funnel

Swimming pool

Propeller

Engine room

Passengers' cabins

The *Norway* can carry 2,400 passengers. There are cabins for the passengers and crew.

There are swimming pools, restaurants, movie theaters, shops, and lounges. Larger cruise ships are being built today.

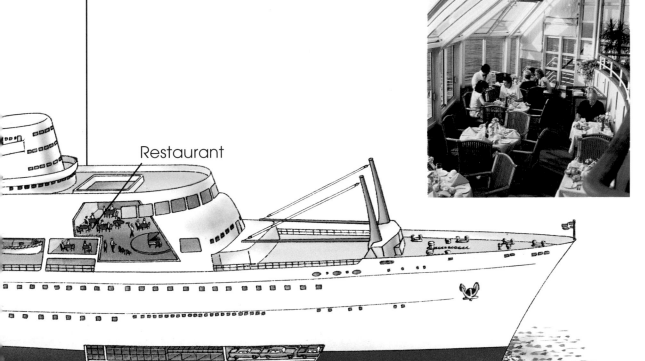

Restaurant

Garage for passengers' cars

Everything that a boat or ship carries is called its cargo. Ships like the one in the picture are very heavy. But they still float. If too many boxes are put on the ship, it will float low in the water. The waves may break over the ship. Then it may sink.

Container ship being loaded

Plimsoll line

Large ships have a mark called the Plimsoll line. There are different lines on it for fresh and salt water. People stop loading the ship when the water comes up to this mark. Otherwise the ship might sink.

Float a margarine tub boat on water. Load your boat with a cargo of marbles or small stones. Add the marbles or stones one by one. What happens if you add too much cargo? Try this activity with a matchbox boat. Will it carry more or less cargo?

Marbles

Margarine tub

Dish pan of cold water

Margarine tub boat

Matchbox boat

23

Hovercraft

There is one type of boat that can move on land and on water. It is called an air cushion vehicle or hovercraft. A hovercraft skims over water or land. It is supported by a cushion of air. This is made by large fans. A rubber skirt keeps the cushion of air in place. The hovercraft is steered by the propellers and rudders. The propellers move around to steer the hovercraft. The rudders also move from side to side to steer it.

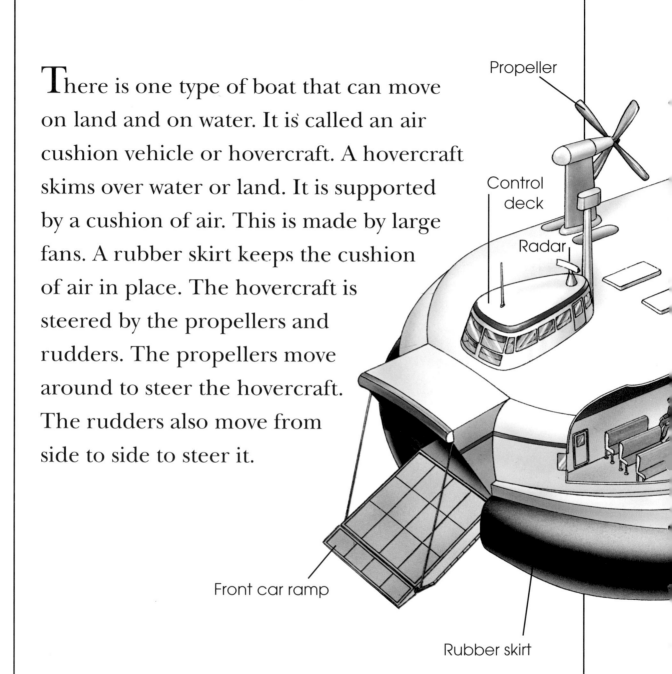

Propeller

Control deck

Radar

Front car ramp

Rubber skirt

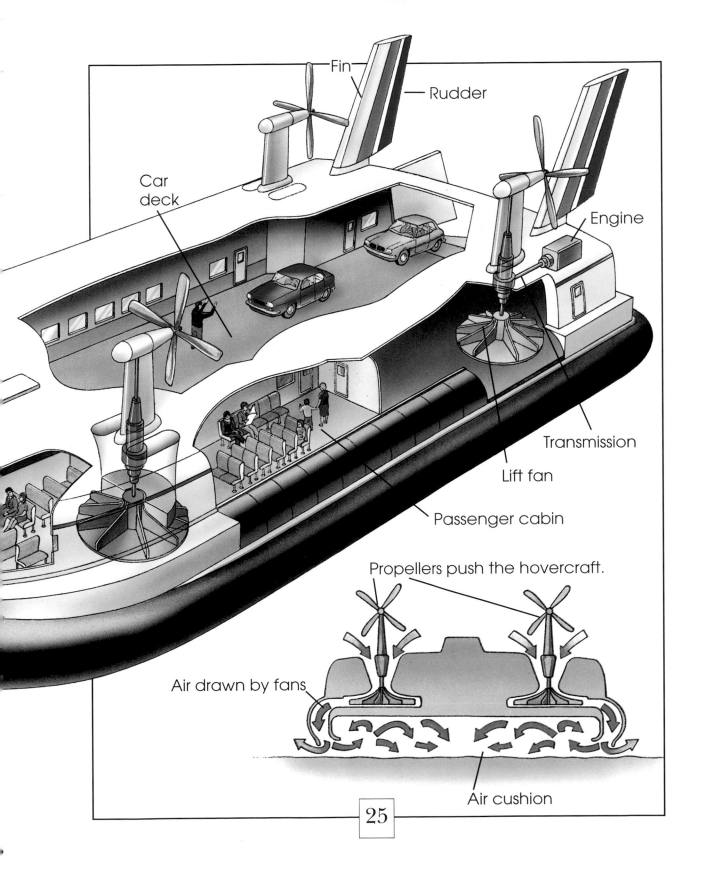

Fin

Rudder

Car deck

Engine

Transmission

Lift fan

Passenger cabin

Propellers push the hovercraft.

Air drawn by fans

Air cushion

25

Make a model hovercraft. Cut a circle from thin cardboard. Make a small hole in the center of the cardboard circle. Ask an adult to make a hole in a cork with a nail. Glue the cork over the hole in the cardboard circle. Make sure the holes line up. Blow up a balloon. Pinch the balloon closed. Carefully stretch the balloon over the cork.

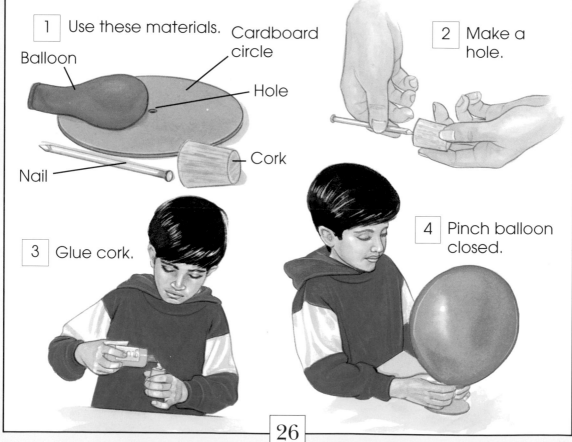

1 Use these materials.

Balloon

Cardboard circle

Hole

Cork

Nail

2 Make a hole.

3 Glue cork.

4 Pinch balloon closed.

Place the hovercraft on a smooth surface. Let go of the balloon and give the hovercraft a little push. Watch what happens.

5 Let go.

Submarines

A submarine can travel under the sea. Submarines have powerful diesel or nuclear engines. To make the submarine go down, it has to become heavier than water. To come up again, it has to become lighter than water.

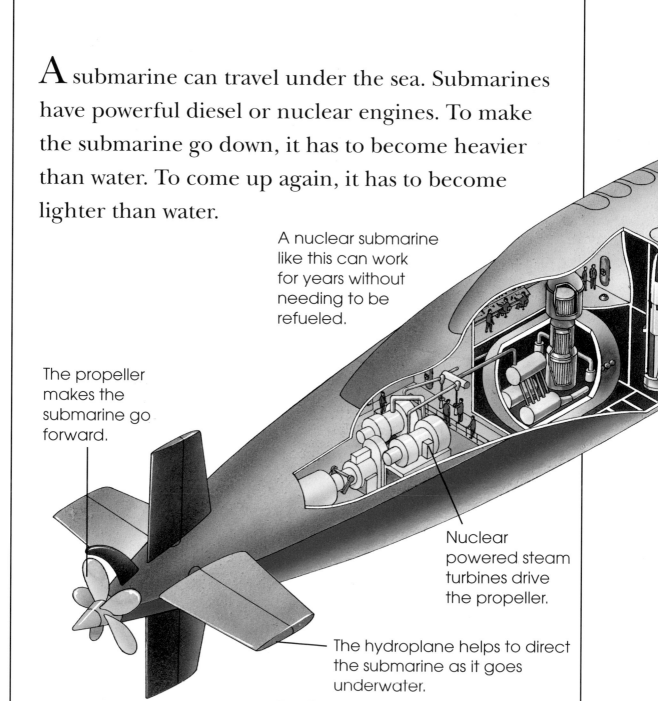

A nuclear submarine like this can work for years without needing to be refueled.

The propeller makes the submarine go forward.

Nuclear powered steam turbines drive the propeller.

The hydroplane helps to direct the submarine as it goes underwater.

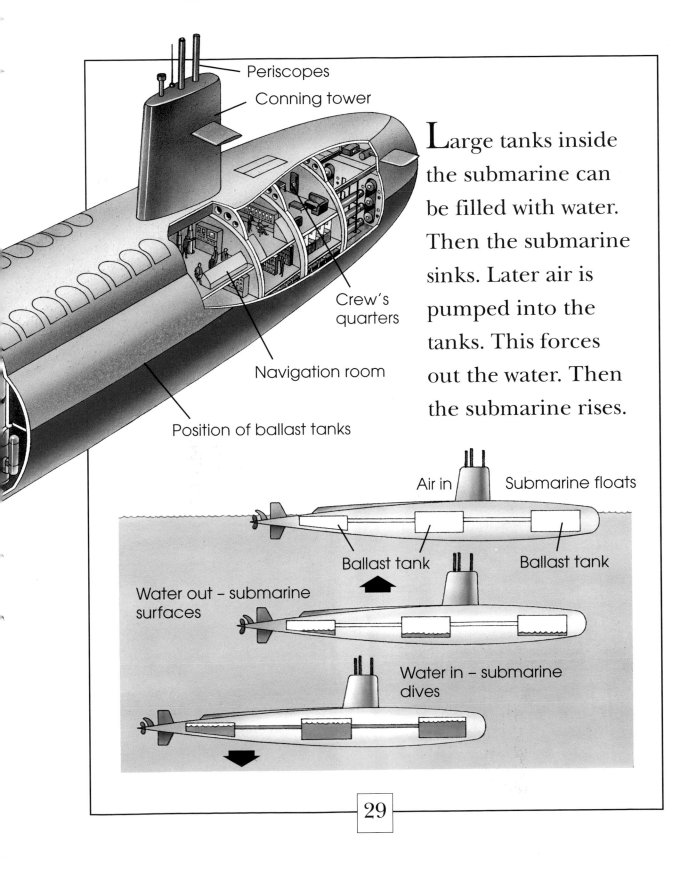

Periscopes

Conning tower

Large tanks inside the submarine can be filled with water. Then the submarine sinks. Later air is pumped into the tanks. This forces out the water. Then the submarine rises.

Crew's quarters

Navigation room

Position of ballast tanks

Air in

Submarine floats

Ballast tank

Ballast tank

Water out – submarine surfaces

Water in – submarine dives

Make a Submarine
See for Yourself

Put a plastic bottle in a bowl of water. Let the bottle fill with water so it sinks. Push one end of a plastic tube into the bottle. Blow into the other end. Can you get the bottom of the bottle to float up to the surface? When the bottle begins to float, squeeze the tube. This will stop the air from getting out. Now your bottle will float like a submarine. To make the bottle sink again, stop squeezing the tube.

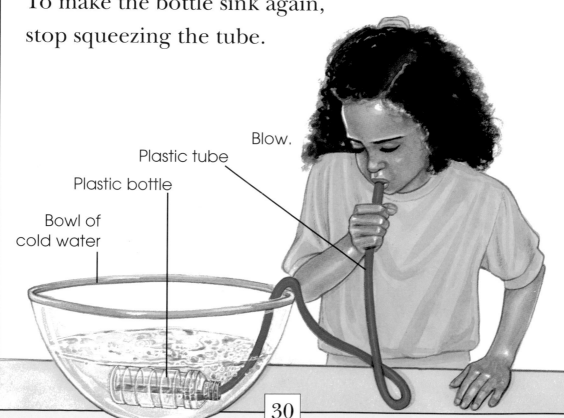

Blow.

Plastic tube

Plastic bottle

Bowl of cold water

30

Glossary

Cargo The goods carried on board a ship.

Catamaran A boat with two hulls.

Float To stay on the surface of water or another liquid.

Hull The body or shell of a ship.

Mast The tall, upright pole to which a boat's sails are attached.

Oar A pole with a flat blade used to row a boat.

Ocean liner A large passenger ship.

Paddle A short oar.

Plimsoll line A line painted on the hull of a cargo ship. It shows the water level to which the ship may be loaded safely.

Propeller A type of fan that turns rapidly to drive a ship along.

Raft A flat floating platform of logs or other materials.

Rudder A flat, hinged piece at the back of a ship, used for steering.

Sail A sheet of material hung from a mast to catch the wind and move a boat forward.

Sink To go down into water or another liquid.

Steel A strong metal made from iron.

Submarine A kind of ship that can travel under the surface of the sea.

Yacht A sailboat built for racing or cruising.

Index

barge 5, 10

canoe 6

cargo 22, 23

catamaran 12–13

container ship 18, 22

coracle 7

cruise liner 4, 5, 20–21

dinghy 5

dugout 7

engine 4, 20, 25, 28

felucca 10

fishing trawler 5

floating 4, 14–15, 16–17, 18–19, 22, 29, 30

Heyerdahl, Thor 9

hovercraft 24–25, 26–27

hull 12, 13, 18

Kon Tiki 9

mast 20

Norway 20–21

oar 4

oil tanker 5

paddle 4

Plimsoll line 22

propeller 20, 24, 25, 28

racing yacht 4, 10

radar 20, 24

raft 6, 8–9

reed boat 6

rudder 25

sail 6, 10, 11

sinking 14–15, 16, 22, 29

steel 16, 18

submarine 28–29, 30

tug 5